Munchie MATH

**Dozens of Skill-Building Math Activities
That Use Edible Manipulatives
to Meet the NCTM Standards**

by Sarah E. Rogers Eckenrode and Linda K. Rogers

NEW YORK • TORONTO • LONDON • AUCKLAND • SYDNEY
MEXICO CITY • NEW DELHI • HONG KONG • BUENOS AIRES

SCHOLASTIC
Teaching
Resources

Thanks to...
Mom, for working with me
Jan, for supporting my ideas in the classroom
—Sarah E. Rogers Eckenrode

Thanks to...
Sarah, who always makes me proud
Denise and "Butch," for their keen eyes and great questions
Jack, who always provides the firm ground beneath my feet
—Linda K. Rogers

Cover design by Norma Ortiz

Interior design by Sydney Wright

Photos by Sarah E. Rogers Eckenrode and Linda K. Rogers

ISBN: 0-439-43828-4
Copyright © 2003 by Sarah E. Rogers Eckenrode and Linda K. Rogers
All rights reserved.
Printed in the U.S.A.

1 2 3 4 5 6 7 8 9 10   40   10 09 08 07 06 05 04 03

Contents

Introduction

Welcome to *Munchie Math*—a delectable way to build essential math skills and meet the standards! Hands-on activities such as Popcorn Count-Up, Crunch 'n' Add, Delicious Dominoes, and A Feast of Fractions use pretzels, cereal, crackers, licorice, and other edible manipulatives to make math learning a treat. You'll find dozens of teacher-tested lessons and student reproducibles to reinforce number sense and help children build skills in addition, subtraction, time, money, patterns, measurement, basic fractions, graphing, and more. If you prefer to use nonedible manipulatives, these activities can easily be adapted without compromising their educational value.

For each lesson, you'll find a clearly stated objective, a list of materials, simple preparation steps, and step-by-step directions to take you through the activity. Many activities include student reproducibles, such as data-collecting sheets, graphs, Bingo boards, number cubes, and more. The activities are organized by the standards outlined by the National Council of Teachers of Mathematics (NCTM): Number and Operations, Algebra, Geometry, Measurement, and Data Analysis. Refer to the Table of Contents to find activities for particular skills.

The activities in the book can be completed in any order and can be adapted as you see fit to meet the needs of your students. For example, if students need additional practice, you might have them return to an activity more than once until you feel they have mastered the concept. You might use an activity from this book each day of the week or you might designate Friday afternoon as "Munchie Math" time. However you choose to implement these activities in your classroom, students are sure to look forward to building math skills with tasty manipulatives on hand.

Munchie Math and the NCTM Standards

Part 1: Number and Operations

In keeping with the recommendations of NCTM for the early primary grades, a major emphasis of *Munchie Math* is Number and Operations. This is the longest section of the book and includes subsections of Number and Number Sense, Operations, Money, and Fractions. During these primary years, children move from basic counting to understanding the size of numbers, number relationships, patterns, operations, and place value. The Number and Operations Standard for prekindergarten through grade 12 states that instructional programs "should enable all students to 1) Understand numbers, ways of representing numbers, relationships among numbers, and number systems; 2) Understand meanings of

operations and how they relate to one another; and 3) Compute fluently and make reasonable estimates" (*Principles and Standards for School Mathematics*, NCTM, 2000). The activities in this section introduce young children to these skills and concepts.

Part 2: Algebra

Algebra for young children does not involve the symbolism taught in later algebra courses, but it does encompass classification, patterns and relation, operations with whole numbers, explorations of function, and step-by-step processes. The Algebra Standard for prekindergarten through grade 12 states that instructional programs "should enable all students to 1) Understand patterns, relations, and functions; 2) Represent and analyze mathematical situations and structures using algebraic symbols; 3) Use mathematical models to represent and understand quantitative relationships; and 4) Analyze change in various contexts" (NCTM, 2000). The activities in this section give children practice in sorting, classifying, and creating patterns.

Part 3: Geometry

The Geometry Standard for prekindergarten through grade 12 states that instructional programs "should enable all students to 1) Analyze characteristics and properties of two- and three-dimensional geometric shapes and develop mathematical arguments about geometric relationships; 2) Specify locations and describe spatial relationships using coordinated geometry and other representational systems; 3) Apply transformations and use symmetry to analyze mathematical situations; and 4) Use visualization, spatial reasoning, and geometric modeling to solve problems" (NCTM, 2000). Teachers can expand children's geometric and spatial knowledge through classroom explorations, investigations, and discussions. In this section, activities engage students in representing two- and three-dimensional shapes with edible materials.

Part 4: Measurement

The Measurement Standard for prekindergarten through grade 12 states that instructional programs "should enable all students to 1) Understand measurable attributes of objects and the units, systems, and processes of measurement; and 2) Apply appropriate techniques, tools, and formulas to determine measurements" (NCTM, 2000). Measurement bridges two areas of mathematics: geometry and number. The activities in this section help children actively engage in measuring through the use of both standard and nonstandard units of measure. Children also compare objects, count units, and make connections between spatial concepts and number as they measure length, weight, volume, and time.

Part 5: Data Analysis

The Data Analysis and Probability Standard for prekindergarten through grade 12 states that instructional programs "should enable all students to 1) Formulate

questions that can be addressed with data and collect, organize, and display relevant data to answer them; 2) Select and use appropriate statistical methods to analyze data; 3) Develop and evaluate inferences and predictions that are based on data; and 4) Understand and apply basic concepts of probability" (NCTM, 2000). Using edible manipulatives provides many opportunities for collecting and analyzing data in the primary classroom. These activities encourage students to pose questions, organize responses, and represent data. (Probability is not included in this section.) Variations are included to provide ways to adapt the activities. As with all of the activities in this book, feel free to make additional changes that will best meet the needs of your students and the requirements of your curriculum.

Teacher Tips

The following suggestions will help facilitate Munchie Math activities in the classroom:

- In advance, read the preparation and procedure steps. Gather necessary supplies and organize them as indicated in the preparation section. Keep some extra snacks on hand.

- Resealable sandwich or snack-sized plastic bags work best for bagging snacks. Provide individual bagged snacks so that only the child who will eat the snack has handled it during the lesson.

- You may want to give children a separate snack to eat rather than have them eat the edible manipulatives used in the math activity.

- If you prefer to use nonedible manipulatives for these activities, you might try buttons, chips, coins, counting bears, dried beans, colored paper squares, eraser tips, and other small, inexpensive items that are available in bulk.

- To create reusable, individual "math mats" for food-related activities, laminate 9- by 12-inch or 12- by 18-inch sheets of construction paper. Thoroughly clean them after each use.

- Before each lesson, have students wash their hands. In addition, you may want to provide antibacterial hand sanitizer or baby wipes on each table.

Safety Note: Before performing food-related activities, check with families about food allergies or dietary restrictions.

- At the beginning of the year, send home a letter to families explaining the purpose of Munchie Math activities. You might request donated supplies and include a list of needed supplies (see sample list on page 8). To reduce costs, you may want to purchase or request snacks in bulk. This is also a good opportunity to invite parent volunteers to visit the classroom and help during Munchie Math time.

■ Scheduling Munchie Math for the last activity on Friday provides a great way to end the week.

■ Before asking children to complete an activity on their own, model the steps for them. You may wish to gather them around a table or use an overhead transparency if the activity includes a reproducible.

■ Most activities can be completed as a class, in small groups, with partners, or individually. While students are working on the activities, walk around the room to check their progress and offer guidance. You might ask students to have you check their work after they have completed the first portion of an activity. This helps ensure that they understand directions and are on the right track.

■ Collect completed reproducibles to assess students' progress and skill levels. Create your own data collection sheets or other reproducibles to use with these activities for additional assessment.

Recommended Edible Manipulatives

Candy

small, multicolored candies, such as
    M&M's® or Skittles®
Red Hots®
multicolored gummy candy,
    such as bears or Swedish Fish®
gumdrops
conversation hearts
thin licorice, such as Twizzlers
    Pull-n-Peel®
jelly beans
candy corn

Cereal

O-shaped cereal, such as Cheerios®
multicolored O-shaped cereal,
    such as Froot Loops®
Lucky Charms®, Honeycomb®,
    Alphabits®, or similar generic-
    brand cereal

Other Snack Items

pretzel sticks and logs
small crackers, such as Cheese
    Nips® or Cheez-It®
animal-shaped crackers
fish-shaped crackers
mini-marshmallows
marshmallows
popcorn
raisins
sunflower seeds

Ordering Snacks

Number and Number Sense

Objective

Students organize objects based on ordinal positions.

Preparation

- Place ten snack items in a bag for each student and the teacher. Each bag must contain the same combination of items (for example, three pretzels, three gumdrops, and four animal crackers).

- Make copies of the reproducible and cut out the paper strips.

- Give each student a bagged snack and a paper strip.

MATERIALS

★ several different snack foods, such as pretzels, gumdrops, and animal-shaped crackers

★ small plastic bags

★ **Ordering Snacks** reproducible (page 16)

Procedure

1. Choose one snack item. Tell students where to place the item on their paper strips by saying an ordinal number—for example, "Place a pretzel in the second square." You might start by giving ordinal numbers in order (first, second, third, and so on).

2. Check students' work for correct placement of items.

3. Once students understand the concept, call out ordinal numbers in a mixed order (fifth, third, tenth, and so on).

Variation

To reinforce ordinal numbers through fifteenth, prepare 2- by 15-inch paper strips and provide students with 15 snack items in plastic bags.

How Many Snacks?

Objectives

Students represent numbers using concrete objects and write numerals.

Preparation

MATERIALS

★ small-sized snack, such as cereal or candy

★ small plastic bags

★ 1-inch oaktag squares

★ permanent marker

★ bag or bowl

★ **Colored Parts** reproducible (page 17)

★ crayons

★ pencils

• Determine which numbers you would like to reinforce. Choose a range of six numbers—for example, 5 to 10. Using a permanent marker, write these numbers on oaktag squares. (You might write the numbers with permanent marker on 1/2-inch ceramic tiles, available at a tile or building-supply store. Sometimes discontinued tiles are free.) Place the number squares in a bag or bowl.

• Place at least 1/4 cup of snack items in a bag for each student. Students will need as many snack items as the greatest number in the range you determined.

• Prepare the Colored Parts reproducible by drawing the same number of columns as the greatest number in the range. (See examples at right for 1–7 and 1–10.) Make a copy for each student.

Name _____	Date _____						
Colored Parts							
Number	**Colored Parts**						

• Give each student a bagged snack, a copy of the reproducible, and at least one crayon and one pencil.

Name _____	Date _____									
Colored Parts										
Number	**Colored Parts**									

Procedure

1. Choose a number square from the bag or bowl. Call out the number and have students place that number of snack items on the bottom row of the worksheet, one snack item per cell (or square). Walk around the room to check students' work and offer assistance.

2. Show students how to draw a mark in each cell containing a snack item. Then have students remove the snacks and color each of the marked cells.

3. Point out the Number column and have students write the numeral in this column.

4. Repeat the procedure until students have filled in every row on the worksheet.

Variation

Instead of using number cards, gather several empty egg cartons. (You will need one for each pair of students.) Write the numerals you are reviewing in the egg carton compartments. Have students work with partners, and give each pair a prepared egg carton. The partners take turns placing a marker in an egg carton, closing the carton, and shaking it. Students then open the carton and identify the numeral where the marker landed. Students place that number of snack items on the bottom row of the Colored Parts sheet, one snack item per cell (or square). The rest of the activity is completed as described in the steps above.

Edible Numerals

Objectives

Students read number words and write numerals from memory.

Preparation

- Determine which numbers you would like to reinforce. Write these number words on index cards. (Laminate the cards for greater durability.)

- You may want to laminate sheets of unlined paper to use as mats for future activities involving food.

- Give each student a sheet of paper as a mat and several thin licorice strips. (If using Twizzlers Pull-n-Peel®, give each student a "rope" of licorice and demonstrate how to "pull and peel" the strips apart. Each rope is made up of several thin strands wrapped together. Note: The candy may break, so students should have more than one string ready before the activity begins.)

Procedure

1 Choose a card and read the number word aloud. Then display the card on the board so students can refer to it.

2 Students use the licorice to form the numeral that represents the number word. Walk around the room to observe students' work.

3 Ask a volunteer to write the numeral on the board next to the word card. Students can check their own numerals.

4 Repeat the procedure until all the number word cards have been used.

MATERIALS

- ★ thin licorice strips, such as Twizzlers Pull-n-Peel® (several thin strips per student)

- ★ 4- by 6-inch index cards

- ★ permanent marker

- ★ 8½- by 11-inch unlined paper

Count and Compare Snacks

Objective

Students use greater than, less than, and equal signs to compare amounts.

Preparation

• Place at least ¹/4 cup of snack items in a bag for each student.

• Give each student a bagged snack and a copy of the reproducible.

Procedure

1 Direct students to grab a small handful of their snack, count the pieces, and record the number of pieces on the reproducible in the column labeled "First Number."

2 Have students repeat step 1, this time recording the number of pieces in the column labeled "Second Number."

3 Students compare the two numbers, then write the greater number in the Greater Number column and the lesser number in the Lesser Number column. If the numbers are equal, the student writes both numbers in the Equal Numbers column.

4 In the last column, have students write a number sentence comparing the two numbers (for example: 8 > 4 or 4 < 8). If the numbers are equal, students write a number sentence such as 6 = 6.

5 Students continue in the same way until they have completed the reproducible.

MATERIALS

★ small-sized snack, such as Cheerios® or other O-shaped cereal

★ small plastic bags

★ **Greater Than/Less Than** reproducible (page 18)

Popcorn Count-Up

Objective

Students count by ones and skip-count by twos, fives, and tens to 100, using manipulatives.

Preparation

- Cut each egg carton so that there are only ten compartments.

- Place at least 100 unpopped popcorn kernels in a bag for each student.

- Give each child an egg carton and a bag of kernels.

Procedure

1. Students count 100 kernels by placing one kernel in a compartment at a time, moving to an adjoining compartment with each kernel. Demonstrate how to place one kernel in one compartment, the second kernel in the next compartment, and so on. Direct students to rotate around the carton again as they count the kernels 11 to 20, and to whisper while counting.

2. Once students have counted to 100, instruct them to pour their leftover kernels, which are still in their plastic bag into a large bowl at the front of the room. Then have them remove their 100 kernels from their egg carton and place them in their now-empty plastic bag.

3. Students count to 100 by twos in the same way, this time picking up two kernels at a time and placing them in one of the compartments. When finished, students can count by fives and tens in the same way. You might end the activity by popping the kernels for a snack. (Use any extra kernals that were not handled in the activity.)

MATERIALS

- ★ popcorn kernels
- ★ small plastic bags
- ★ empty egg cartons
- ★ large bowl
- ★ hot-air popcorn popper (optional)

Cereal Place Value

Objective

Students represent numerals in the tens place and the ones place.

Preparation

- Place at least $1/4$ cup of the small cereal and $1/4$ cup of the medium-sized cereal in a bag for each student.

- Determine the range of numbers to be used.

- Give each student a bagged snack, a copy of the reproducible, and a pencil. (Glue is optional.)

Procedure

Model the steps for students first. You may want to create an overhead transparency of the reproducible.

1 Choose a number card and read it aloud. Students place medium-sized cereal pieces in the Tens column of the reproducible to represent the number in the tens place of the number chosen. Explain that one medium-sized cereal piece represents ten small cereal pieces. For example, for 43, students would place four medium-sized cereal pieces in the Tens column. (If desired, have students glue the pieces onto the worksheet.)

2 Students place small cereal pieces in the Ones column to represent the number in the ones place. For 43, students would place three small cereal pieces in the Ones column.

3 Students write the two-digit numeral in the Number column. Repeat until students have filled in their worksheets.

MATERIALS

- ★ small-sized cereal, such as Cheerios® or other O-shaped cereal
- ★ medium-sized cereal, such as Honeycomb®
- ★ small plastic bags
- ★ pencils
- ★ **Place Value** reproducible (page 19)
- ★ number cards or tiles
- ★ glue (optional)

Ordering Snacks

Name _____

Date _____

Colored Parts

Number	Colored Parts					

Name _____

Date _____

Greater Than/Less Than

First Number	Second Number	Greater Number	Lesser Number	Equal Numbers	> Greater Than < Less Than = Equal To

Name _____

Date _____

Place Value

Tens	Ones	Number

Poppin' for Addition

MATERIALS

- ★ popcorn or other small-sized snack
- ★ small plastic bags
- ★ number cube and blank cube (page 31) or die
- ★ **Addition or Subtraction** reproducible (page 30)

Variation

To practice subtraction, have students roll number cubes or dice, then record the larger numeral in the first box and the smaller numeral in the second box. Ask students what symbol should be written to show subtraction of the two numerals. Place the "−" sign in the appropriate position. Use snack pieces as manipulatives to represent the two numerals and solve the problem. Record the difference in the third box.

Objective

Students create and solve addition problems with sums to 20.

Preparation

- Determine the range of numbers to be used. You may use a die or number cube for numbers 1 to 6. If you use other numbers, write these on the blank cube template (page 31).
- Place at least 1/4 cup of snack items in a bag for each student. The amount you need depends on the numbers used in the addition problems.
- Give each student a bagged snack, a number cube, and a copy of the reproducible.

Procedure

Model the steps first. You may want to create an overhead transparency of the reproducible for the demonstration.

1. Roll the number cube. On the reproducible, record the numeral rolled in the first box in the first row. Repeat, recording the second numeral in the second box in the first row.

2. Ask students what symbol should be written to show addition of the two numbers. Place the "+" sign in the appropriate position. Use snack pieces as manipulatives to represent the two numerals, and solve the problem. Place the snacks on the reproducible or another clean sheet of paper.

3. Students continue until all rows are completed.

A Bite of Bingo

Objective

Students solve addition problems with sums to 20.

Preparation

- Place at least $1/4$ cup of snack items in a bag for each student.

- Determine the range of sums you will be using in this activity. Write addition problems on index cards with those sums. (For a subtraction activity, write subtraction problems.)

- Create a Bingo board for each student by filling in the squares with the sums of the addition problems. Be sure to make each card different. Laminate the boards for greater durability.

- Give each student a bagged snack and a Bingo board.

Procedure

1. Select an index card and read aloud the addition problem on it. Write the problem on the board.

2. Students solve the problem and look for the sum on their Bingo boards. If students find the answer, they place a snack item on that square.

3. Continue to read and record problems until a student calls out "Bingo!" This student should have a horizontal, vertical, or diagonal row covered with pieces.

4. Have the student read the sums marked on his or her board. Refer to the problems on the board to check the student's answers. Students may clear their boards by eating the snack pieces before you begin a new game.

MATERIALS

- ★ small-sized snack, such as cereal or raisins
- ★ small plastic bags
- ★ index cards
- ★ permanent marker
- ★ **Bingo** board reproducible (page 32)

Crunch 'n' Add

Objective

Students complete continuous addition with regrouping, "trading" ones for tens until they reach a sum of 100.

Preparation

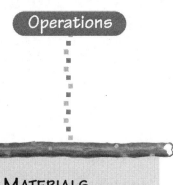

MATERIALS

★ pretzel sticks and pretzel logs

★ small plastic bags

★ die or number cube (page 31)

★ **Tens and Ones** reproducible (page 33)

• Place twenty pretzel sticks and ten pretzel logs in a bag for each student.

• Give each student a bagged snack and a copy of the reproducible.

• Have students work with a partner, sitting side by side. Each pair will need one die or number cube.

Procedure

Model the procedure first. You may want to create an overhead transparency of the reproducible.

1. To take a turn, a player rolls the die and places that number of pretzel sticks on the ones side of the reproducible. On the next turn, the player rolls the die again and adds that number of pretzel sticks to the ones side.

2. If the total number of pretzel sticks is greater than or equal to ten, the player trades the ten pretzel sticks for one pretzel log. He or she returns the sticks to the bag, retrieves a log, and places the pretzel log on the tens side of the worksheet.

3. Players continue to take turns rolling the die and placing that many pretzel sticks on the ones side. When there are ten or more sticks, the player trades them for a log.

4. The first student to reach or exceed 100 by trading all of his or her pretzel sticks for ten logs tallies a win. Students can return the sticks and logs to their bags and play again.

Pretzel Addition

Objectives

Students solve two-digit addition problems with regrouping. Students determine whether regrouping is required.

Preparation

- Place at least twenty pretzel sticks and ten pretzel logs in a bag for each student.

- Determine the two-digit numbers to be used in the addition problems. (You might shuffle number cards or place number tiles in a bowl to ensure random selection during the activity.)

- Give each student a bagged snack and a copy of the reproducible.

Procedure

Model the procedure for this activity twice. You may want to create an overhead transparency of the reproducible.

1 For the first problem, select two number cards that can be added together without regrouping (for example, 11 + 13).

2 Record the first numeral in the top box of problem 1 on the reproducible. Use the pretzel logs to represent tens and pretzel sticks to represent ones. Explain that one log represents ten sticks. (To represent 11, for example, you would use 1 log and 1 stick.) Place the pretzels on the reproducible or another clean sheet of paper.

3 Record the second numeral in the second box of problem 1. Again, use pretzel logs and sticks to represent this numeral. (To represent 13, for example, you would use 1 log and 3 sticks.)

MATERIALS

- ★ pretzel sticks
- ★ pretzel logs
- ★ small plastic bags
- ★ number cards or tiles (10–99)
- ★ **Vertical Addition or Subtraction** reproducible (page 34)

23

4 Ask students which operation sign should be used to add the two numerals. Write a "+" sign to the left of the second box. Add the ones by counting the total number of pretzel sticks. Record this number in the ones place in the answer box. Add the tens by counting the total number of pretzel logs. Record this number in the tens place of the answer box. Read the whole problem.

5 For the second problem, select two numbers that require regrouping to find the sum, such as 18 + 16. Repeat the steps above. When you are ready to determine the total number of ones, remind students that 9 is the greatest number they can write in the ones place.

6 Trade ten pretzel sticks (10 ones) for one pretzel log (1 ten). To solve 18 + 16, you would have 2 logs and 14 sticks. Trade 10 of the sticks for 1 log. You would then have 3 logs and 4 sticks. Record the number of sticks in the ones place and the number of logs in the tens place. Read the problem aloud.

7 Randomly draw two number cards or tiles for the third problem. Ask students to tell you the steps to solve the problem, and have them determine whether trading is necessary to add the ones. Encourage students to provide reasons for the steps. Ask a volunteer to manipulate the pretzel sticks and logs and record the answers.

8 Once students are ready to work independently, draw number cards and write the numbers for each problem on the transparency or on the chalkboard. Have students work with their own pretzels and solve the problems until all rows are completed.

Pretzel Subtraction

Objectives

Students solve two-digit subtraction problems with regrouping. Students determine whether regrouping is required.

Preparation

- Place at least twenty pretzel sticks and ten pretzel logs in a bag for each student.

- Write a variety of two-digit subtraction problems on index cards, including several that require regrouping.

- Give each student a bagged snack and a copy of the reproducible.

Procedure

Model the procedure for this activity twice. You may wish to create an overhead transparency of the reproducible.

1 For the first problem, select a subtraction problem that does not require regrouping to solve (for example, 23 – 11).

2 Record the first numeral in the top box of problem 1 on the reproducible. Use pretzel logs to represent tens and pretzel sticks to represent ones. Explain that one log represents ten sticks. (For example, to represent 23, you would use 2 logs and 3 sticks.) Place the pretzels on the reproducible or another clean sheet of paper.

3 Record the second numeral in the second box of problem 1. Again, use pretzel logs and sticks to represent this numeral. (To represent 11, you would use 1 log and 1 stick.)

4 Ask students which operation sign should be used to subtract the second numeral from the first. Write a "−" sign to the left of the second box.

MATERIALS

- ★ pretzel sticks and pretzel logs
- ★ small plastic bags
- ★ index cards
- ★ permanent marker
- ★ **Vertical Addition or Subtraction** reproducible (page 34)

5 To subtract the ones, first count the number of pretzel sticks for the top numeral. Ask students how many ones should be subtracted or "taken away" (the number in the ones place of the second numeral). Remove that number of pretzel sticks. Ask students how many pretzel sticks are left. Record this numeral in the ones place in the answer box. Repeat the process with the tens column, using the pretzel logs. Read the whole problem.

6 For the second problem, select a subtraction problem that requires regrouping to solve (for example, 23 – 15). Repeat the steps above. When you are ready to subtract the ones, remind students that the number of ones on top must be greater than the number of ones on the bottom.

7 Look at the numeral in the top box and the pretzels representing this number. For example, for 23, you would have 2 logs and 3 sticks. Trade 1 pretzel log (1 ten) for 10 pretzel sticks (10 ones). Now you should have 1 log and 13 sticks. To subtract the ones, remove the appropriate number of sticks and record the difference in the ones place. To subtract the tens, remove the appropriate number of logs and record the number in the tens place. Read the whole problem.

8 Select another subtraction problem. Ask students to tell you the steps to follow to solve the problem, and have them determine whether trading is necessary to subtract the ones. Encourage students to provide reasons for the steps. Ask a volunteer to manipulate the pretzels and record the answers.

9 Once students are ready to work independently, write subtraction problems on the transparency or on the chalkboard. Have students work with their own pretzels and solve the problems until they have completed all problems on the worksheet.

Delicious Dominoes

Operations

Objective

Students write addition sentences with sums to 20.

Preparation

- Place at least ¹/4 cup of snack items in a bag for each student.

- Create a poster or overhead that shows one or more patterns of domino dots from 1 to 9 (one example shown at right). Or, provide a set of dominoes.

- Draw a horizontal midline on each index card to create a blank domino.

- Give each student a bagged snack, five to ten index cards, and glue.

MATERIALS

- ★ small, uniform-sized snack, such as Cheerios® or other O-shaped cereal, or Red Hots®
- ★ small plastic bags
- ★ glue
- ★ 4- by 6-inch index cards
- ★ permanent marker
- ★ lined paper

Procedure

1. Have students examine the configuration of dots on a set of dominoes or on the poster or transparency you created.

2. Show students how to glue snack items onto index cards to create domino cards. You may want students to create any numbers they wish, or you may direct them to create certain numbers. Once students have finished making their domino cards, they may eat the snack remaining in their bags.

3. Model how to use the domino cards to create addition problems. Have students write and solve an addition sentence for each domino they created (and more if time allows). Students may also trade dominoes with a partner and write other addition sentences. Students may also create subtraction problems.

Safety Note: Remind students not to eat the snacks during this activity since they are using glue. If desired, set aside a separate snack for students to eat when they are finished with this activity.

Subtraction-Story Snack Problems

MATERIALS

* ★ snacks with specific shapes, such as fish-shaped crackers, Swedish Fish®, gummy candies, or animal-shaped crackers

* ★ small plastic bags

* ★ **Vertical Addition or Subtraction** reproducible (page 34)

* ★ index cards

* ★ permanent marker

Challenge students to write and solve their own addition- and subtraction-story problems.

Objective

Students write subtraction sentences and solve word problems.

Preparation

• Place at least $1/4$ cup of snack items in a bag for each student.

• Create subtraction flash cards (such as $16 - 7$). On the index cards, create simple word problems to illustrate the subtraction problems. (For example: *Jenny had 16 crackers in her lunch bag. The bag had a hole. She lost 7 crackers. How many crackers did Jenny have left?*)

• Give each student a bagged snack and a copy of the reproducible.

Procedure

1 Select an index card, read the problem, and model how to think aloud about it. You may want to make an overhead transparency of the reproducible, or write the problem on the chalkboard.

2 Ask students what sign to place in the problem, and write a subtraction sign in the appropriate place. Use snack items to illustrate the problem and then solve it.

3 Select another flash card and read the problem. Ask a student volunteer to record the problem on the transparency worksheet and think aloud to solve it.

4 Continue to select index cards, read problems, and allow students to solve the problems independently. Ask volunteers to share their solutions.

Fact Families

Objective

Students use three numbers to create fact families.

Preparation

- Determine the fact families you would like students to practice.

- Place snack items in a bag for each student. The number of pieces should be equal to the largest number you would like to use in this activity.

- Give each student a bagged snack and a Fact Families reproducible.

Procedure

1 Review fact families with students, such as 6 + 2 = 8, 2 + 6 = 8, 8 − 2 = 6, and 8 − 6 = 2. You may want to make a transparency of the reproducible.

2 Grab a handful of snack items and record the total number of snack items (such as 10) in the top box of the first problem on the reproducible.

3 Divide this amount of snack items into two piles (for example, 4 and 6). Record these two numbers in the two boxes beneath the total number.

4 Create two addition problems using these two numbers (such as 4 + 6 = 10 and 6 + 4 = 10). Record the problems on the lines. Then create two subtraction problems using the numbers (such as 10 − 4 = 6 and 10 − 6 = 4). Record these on the lines.

5 Have students work independently until they have filled in all of the boxes on their worksheets.

MATERIALS

- ★ uniform-sized snack, such as crackers, cereal, or raisins
- ★ small plastic bags
- ★ **Fact Families** reproducible (page 35)

10	
4	6

4 + 6 = 10
6 + 4 = 10
10 − 4 = 6
10 − 6 = 4

Name _____   Date _____

Addition or Subtraction

1   ☐   ☐   =   ☐

2   ☐   ☐   =   ☐

3   ☐   ☐   =   ☐

4   ☐   ☐   =   ☐

5   ☐   ☐   =   ☐

6   ☐   ☐   =   ☐

7   ☐   ☐   =   ☐

8   ☐   ☐   =   ☐

9   ☐   ☐   =   ☐

10 ☐   ☐   =   ☐

Name _____

Date _____

Number Cubes

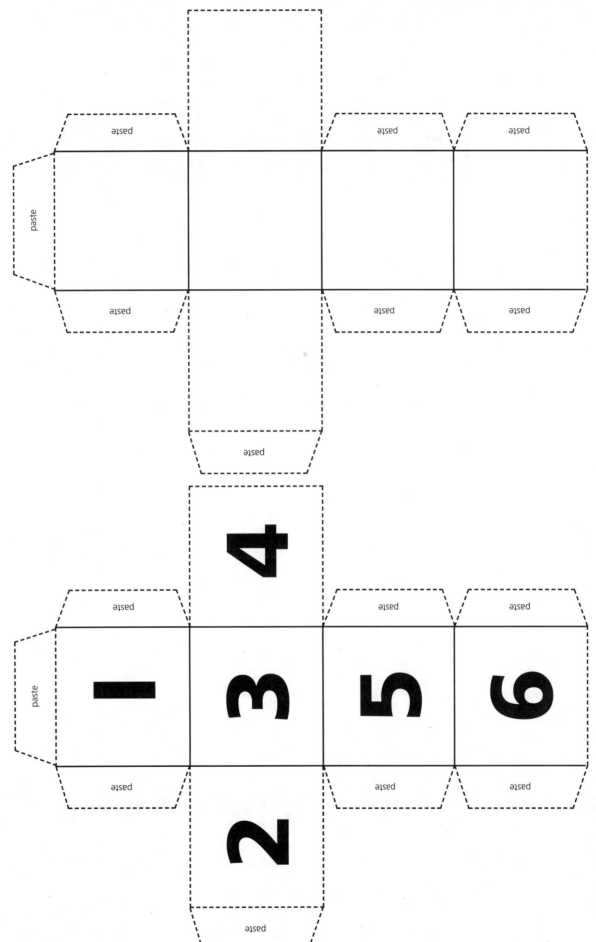

Name _____   Date _____

BINGO

Name _____

Date _____

Tens and Ones

Tens	Ones

Name _____

Date _____

Vertical Addition or Subtraction

1

2

3

4

5

6

7

8

9

10

Fact Families

1

2

3

4

5

6

Coin Bingo

Objective

Students identify United States coins by their visual characteristics.

Preparation

• Place at least ¹/4 cup of snack items in a bag for each student.

• Make several copies of the Coins reproducible and cut apart the coin cards.

• Give each student a bagged snack, glue, a copy of the Bingo board, and approximately 20 coin cards. Keep a teacher pile of about 20 coin cards.

Procedure

MATERIALS

★ small-sized snack, such as cereal or raisins

★ small plastic bags

★ glue

★ **Bingo** board reproducible (page 32)

★ **Coins** reproducible (page 41)

1 Have students glue one coin card in each square of their Bingo board in random order. They should not make their Bingo board the same as anyone sitting near them.

2 Choose a coin card from the teacher pile and call it out by giving a visual clue. For example, for a nickel you might say: "The coin worth five cents" or "The coin with Thomas Jefferson on it." You might even be specific about which side of a coin students should look for, such as "The heads side of a nickel." Keep track of how many times you have called each coin.

3 Students look for that coin on their Bingo boards and place a piece of snack food on that coin if it is found.

4 When a student has completed a vertical, horizontal, or diagonal row, he or she calls out "Bingo!" Have the student describe the coins in his or her completed row. Students can then clear their boards by eating the snack pieces.

Color-Coded Coins

Money

Objective

Students read a chart and add the monetary value of mixed coins.

Preparation

- Place at least ¼ cup of snack items in a bag for each student.

- Use colored markers on chart paper to create a color-coded chart. On the chart, assign each color of snack items a coin value. You may want to use snack foods in three different shapes, such as gummy bears, gummy fish, and gummy fruits.

    Example of a color-coded chart:
    red = penny
    yellow = nickel
    green = dime

- Give each student a bagged snack, crayons, and a copy of the reproducible.

MATERIALS

- ★ multicolored snack, such as Froot Loops®, gummy candy, or Skittles®
- ★ small plastic bags
- ★ chart paper
- ★ colored markers
- ★ **Color-Coded Money** reproducible (page 42)
- ★ crayons

Procedure

1. Explain the color-coded chart to students. Then model the procedure using a copy of the worksheet or an overhead transparency.

2. Remove three or four colored snack pieces from the bag. Think aloud as you refer to the color-coded chart to line up the snack pieces from greatest to least value. Place one piece in each box labeled "Color," keeping the pieces in the same order from greatest to least value. For example, using the chart above, you would line up the following snack pieces in this order: green, yellow, red, red.

3 Refer to the color-coded chart and write the value of each snack piece in the box directly below it. For example, you would write 10¢ beneath a green snack item.

4 Add the snacks' monetary value to determine their total value. Record this amount at the end of the row.

5 As you remove each snack piece, color the box the same color as the snack.

6 Have students follow the steps independently to fill in the rest of the worksheet. Explain that they may choose up to 8 pieces in each handful. If they take more than this amount, they can return the extra pieces to the bag. You might allow children to eat the snack pieces as they remove them from the worksheet.

Variation

To play Money Pull, students work on the above activity in pairs. The first player pulls several snack items from his or her bag and adds up their monetary value. The second player then pulls snack items from his or her bag, hoping to have a selection with a greater monetary value than the first player's selection. The player whose snacks have a greater monetary value wins the round. Players can determine in advance how many rounds they will play. Students can play this game with or without the reproducible.

Coin Tally

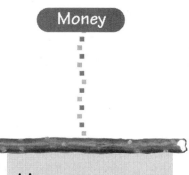

Objective

Students identify and add the value of coins.

Preparation

- Place at least 1/4 cup of snack items in a bag for each student.
- Divide the class into groups of no more than four students.
- Give each student a bagged snack and a copy of the Coin Tally reproducible. Give each group a coin cube.
- Determine the amount of money students' bagged snack is worth or have students determine an amount (such as $.50). Add a price tag with the same amount to each bag. Make sure each price is high enough so that students will need to roll the cube several times in order to reach or exceed the price.

Procedure

1. Each player takes a turn rolling the coin cube and making a tally mark in the appropriate box on his or her reproducible to show what was rolled.

2. In the next round of turns, each player rolls the cube, makes a tally mark, and then adds up the monetary value of both tally marks. The player writes this amount at the bottom of his or her reproducible.

3. Players continue to take turns, recording a new total monetary amount on each turn. The first player to have enough money to "buy" the bagged snack wins. (The other players check that this player has added correctly.)

MATERIALS

- ★ any snack, such as cereal or raisins
- ★ small plastic bags
- ★ **Coin Tally** reproducible (page 43)
- ★ **Coin Cubes** reproducible (page 44)

Money

Shopping for Snacks

Objective

Students add the value of coins and "shop" for snacks in a classroom store.

Preparation

• Ask families to donate bagged snacks to be placed in a "classroom store."

• Determine prices for store items and make a price tag for each.

• Set up tables with store items. You might invite parent volunteers to act as vendors.

• Determine how much "money" students will have to spend at the store. Give each student scissors and a copy of the reproducible. Have students cut apart their coins and count the amount determined. The leftover coins can be used as change for the vendors. If you need more change, make additional copies of the Coins reproducible.

Procedure

MATERIALS

★ **Coins** reproducible (page 41)

★ bagged snacks (any kind)

★ scissors

1. Discuss appropriate behavior when "shopping" in the classroom store. Explain the procedures of how to browse, make decisions, and purchase items.

2. Determine what time the store will open. At that time, have students walk around the store and shop.

3. Have students take responsibility for counting their own coins to pay for their purchases. When they have made their decisions, students pay the vendor for the items.

4. When shopping is complete, students may sit together and enjoy their purchases.

Coins

Name _____

Date _____

Color-Coded Money

	=
Color	**Amount**

	=
Color	**Amount**

	=
Color	**Amount**

	=
Color	**Amount**

Name _____   Date _____

Coin Tally

penny	nickel
dime	quarter 

Money amount _____

Name _____

Date _____

Coin Cubes

paste

paste

paste

paste

paste

paste

paste

paste

paste

paste

paste

paste

ONE CENT · UNITED STATES OF AMERICA

LIBERTY · 1985 · IN GOD WE TRUST

IN GOD WE TRUST · LIBERTY · 1985

E PLURIBUS UNUM · MONTICELLO · FIVE CENTS · UNITED STATES OF AMERICA

UNITED STATES OF AMERICA · E PLURIBUS UNUM

LIBERTY · 1985 · IN GOD WE TRUST

LIBERTY · 1985

UNITED STATES OF AMERICA · ONE DIME

E PLURIBUS UNUM · MONTICELLO · FIVE CENTS · UNITED STATES OF AMERICA

IN GOD WE TRUST · LIBERTY · 1985

LIBERTY · 1985 · IN GOD WE TRUST

Creating Fractions

Objective

Students cut foods to represent basic fractions.

Preparation

- Determine the fractions you would like to reinforce ($1/2$, $1/4$, and $1/8$ work well for this activity) and write these on chart paper or on the chalkboard.

- Separate the licorice ropes. (If using Twizzlers Pull-n-Peel®, each rope contains nine strings. Each student will need one or two ropes, depending on the length of the activity.) Place each student's rope(s) on a paper plate.

- You may want to laminate sheets of unlined paper to use as mats for future activities involving food.

- Give each student a paper plate with licorice rope(s), a sheet of paper as a mat, and a plastic knife (optional).

Procedure

1. Have students carefully separate the strings of licorice in the rope and set aside the pieces on the paper plate.

2. Lead a class discussion about how to cut a piece of licorice to show a given fraction. Gather students around or use an overhead projector. Think aloud about how many equal pieces you will cut to represent the fraction. For example, to create $1/2$, you will cut only one time, dividing the string into two equal pieces. Explain that each piece represents one half of the whole.

MATERIALS

- ★ thin licorice, such as Twizzlers Pull-n-Peel®
- ★ plastic knives (optional; see safety note below)
- ★ paper plates
- ★ $8^{1}/2$- by 11-inch unlined paper

Safety Note: If you feel using plastic knives is problematic, students can pinch the licorice to cut it instead. Demonstrate how to do this at the beginning of the activity.

3 Have students place one licorice string on the mat and tell them to cut the licorice to show a particular fraction. Guide students as they either cut or pinch the string. Help students experiment with folding the strings before they cut so the pieces are as equal as possible.

4 Continue until all fractions have been created.

Variations

⊚ To create an assessment sheet, list questions such as "How many cuts did you make to create halves? To create thirds? Fourths?" Draw a piece of licorice for each question so children can draw where they made the cuts.

⊚ Use other snack items to create fractions. Choose items that students are able to cut easily, such as slices of bread, bananas, or soft cookies. (If you use a food that is more difficult to cut, demonstrate the cutting rather than having students do it.) Or choose items that don't need to be cut, such as a bag of cereal or raisins that can be divided evenly into halves, fourths, and eighths.

A Feast of Fractions

Objective

Students use colorful snacks to represent and name fractional parts of a whole.

Preparation

• Place at least fifty snack pieces in a bag for each student.

• Give each student a bagged snack, a copy of the reproducible, and crayons that are the same colors as the snack.

Procedure

Model the steps for students first.

1 Count eight pieces of cereal or candy. Place one piece in each "slice" of the first circle on the worksheet.

2 On each slice, make a dot that is the same color as the piece of candy or cereal on that slice. Remove the snacks and use the dots as a guide for coloring the slices.

3 Lead a discussion about the fractional parts of the circle. Ask students questions, such as:

• How many parts make up the circle?

• How many parts are blue?

• How many parts are red?

• Which color has the most parts?

4 Model how a fraction is written. Write fractions to show the answers to the questions you have discussed.

MATERIALS

★ small, multicolored cereal or candy, such as Froot Loops® or M&M's®

★ small plastic bags

★ crayons (same colors as snack)

★ **Fraction Circles** reproducible (page 49)

5 Ask students to complete the first circle on their worksheets in the same way. Walk around the room to check students' work and offer assistance. Ask students questions to help them think about the fractional parts of their circles. Encourage them to discuss their findings with a classmate.

6 Once students have successfully completed the first circle, have them repeat the steps and color the rest of the circles on the worksheet. Encourage them to use a different arrangement of colors on each.

Variations

◉ Create an assessment sheet that lists questions such as:

- In circle 1, how many parts are blue? How would you write this as a fraction?

- In circle 2, which color covers the most parts?

- Which circle has the most parts that are red?

◉ Place colored snack items on a strip of paper that is divided into equal squares. Have students name the fractional parts of the whole.

◉ String colored O-shaped cereal (such as Froot Loops®) on a piece of yarn and tie the ends together. Ask students to name the fractional parts of the whole.

Name _____

Date _____

Fraction Circles

2

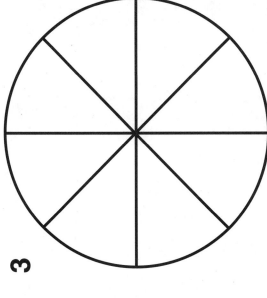

3

1

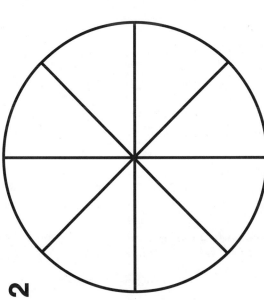

4

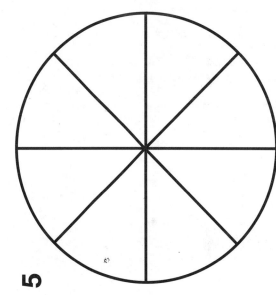

5

6

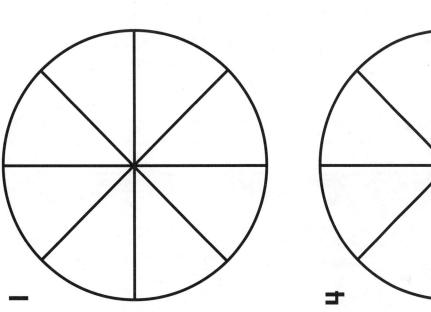

Cereal Sorting

MATERIALS

★ cereal or other snack that can be sorted by attributes*

★ small plastic bags

★ 8 1/2- by 11-inch unlined paper

* Multicolored cereal or candies such as Froot Loops®, Skittles®, M&M's®, and jelly beans are all good choices for sorting by color. Lucky Charms® can be sorted by shape. Alpha-Bits® cereal can be sorted by vowels and consonants. For sorting by size, mix different sized cereals or candies.

Objective

Students sort cereal or other snacks based on visual attributes.

Preparation

- Select an appropriate snack based on whether you want students to sort by color, size, shape, or some other attribute.

- Place at least 1/4 cup of cereal in a bag for each student.

- You may want to laminate sheets of unlined paper to use as mats for future activities involving food.

- Give each student a bagged snack and a sheet of paper as a mat.

Procedure

1 Gather students around and pour a bagged snack onto a mat for a demonstration. Ask students to help you decide how to sort it. Model the way you want students to sort the snack.

2 Have students return to their seats. Ask them to determine how they will sort their snacks.

3 Walk around the room checking students' work and asking them to explain how they sorted their snacks.

4 Once students are finished sorting, invite them to share their sorting rationale with the class.

Food Patterns

Sorting and Creating Patterns

Objective

Students extend AB, ABC, ABBC, and/or AABB patterns using snacks of different colors.

Preparation

- Determine which patterns you would like students to extend and select an appropriate multicolored snack.
- Place at least 1/4 cup of snack items in a bag for each student.
- Give each student a bagged snack, crayons, and a copy of the reproducible.

Procedure

1. Discuss the characteristics of each pattern (AB, ABC, ABBC, AABB). On the chalkboard, demonstrate how to create one of the patterns by using shapes, colors, letters, or numbers.

2. Gather students around. Model how to use the snack items to create one of the patterns on the Basic Patterns reproducible. For an AB pattern, choose two colors to alternate in the squares in that row. Complete the pattern, share it with the class, and then color the squares as you remove the snack pieces.

3. Have students create their own AB pattern on their sheets and then color the squares with crayons.

4. Instruct students to work on the next patterns in the same way. After students create the patterns with snack pieces and have their work checked, they should color the squares.

5. Invite students to create their own patterns using their snack. They can either eat the snack when finished or glue the pieces onto the paper.

MATERIALS

- ★ multicolored snack, such as Froot Loops®, Skittles®, or M&M's®
- ★ small plastic bags
- ★ **Basic Patterns** reproducible (page 54)
- ★ crayons
- ★ glue (optional)

Growing Patterns

Objective

Students create growing patterns using snacks of different colors.

Growing Patterns reproducible (page 55)

MATERIALS

* ✶ multicolored snack, such as Froot Loops® or M&M's®
* ✶ small plastic bags
* ✶ **Growing Patterns** reproducible (page 55)
* ✶ crayons
* ✶ scissors
* ✶ 12- by 18-inch construction paper
* ✶ glue

Preparation

• Determine which patterns you would like students to practice (AB, ABC, ABBC, AABB, and so on) and write these on the chalkboard. Then select an appropriate snack.

• Place at least ¹/4 cup of snack items in a bag for each student.

• Give each student a bagged snack, a sheet of construction paper, crayons, scissors, glue, and a copy of the reproducible.

Procedure

1. Explain the difference between a repeating pattern and a growing pattern. Provide examples of each, such as:
    A B A B A B A B (repeating)
    A B A A B A A A B A A A A B (growing)
    Review how to create a growing pattern on the chalkboard (one part of the pattern stays the same while the other part grows). Ask volunteers to create colored patterns with chalk.

2. Demonstrate how to cut apart the strips of boxes on the reproducible, then paste two strips together to create one long strip. Model how to create a given pattern using snack pieces on a strip. Discuss and show how to make the pattern "grow." Then remove each snack piece and color the square beneath it the same color.

3. Have students use snacks to create the growing patterns written on the chalkboard. Ask them to show you their snack pattern before they color their strips. You might challenge them to create their own growing patterns as well. When students are finished, they can glue their strips onto construction paper.

Pattern Necklaces

Objective

Students create a repeating-pattern necklace using colorful cereal pieces.

Preparation

- Place at least ¹/2 cup of snack items in a bag for each student.

- Tie a large knot on one end of each piece of yarn and wrap tape around the other end.

- You may want to laminate sheets of unlined paper to use as mats for future activities involving food.

- Determine what type of pattern students should choose from (AB, ABC, ABBC, AABB) for this activity.

- Give each student a piece of yarn, a bagged snack, and a sheet of paper as a mat.

Procedure

1. Review several types of patterns, such as AB, ABC, ABBC, and AABB. Have students use different colored pieces of cereal to show each pattern on their mats.

2. Explain that students will be creating pattern necklaces. Each student will decide on a pattern and repeat it at least five times on his or her necklace. Have students arrange their cereal pieces in order on their mats before stringing them onto the yarn.

3. Walk around the room to check students' work and offer assistance. Once students have strung their patterns correctly, help them tie the string ends together to create a necklace.

MATERIALS

- ★ multicolored O-shaped cereal, such as Froot Loops®
- ★ small plastic bags
- ★ 24- to 30-inch pieces of yarn
- ★ tape
- ★ 8¹/2- by 11-inch unlined paper

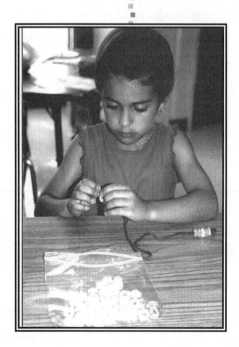

Name _____

Date _____

Basic Patterns

AB							

ABC							

ABBC							

AABB							

Your Own							

Growing Patterns

paste	

paste	

paste	

Creating Shapes

Objective

Students create basic two-dimensional shapes with edible materials.

Preparation

• Separate the licorice "ropes."

• You may want to laminate sheets of unlined paper to use as mats for future activities involving food.

• Give each student a paper plate with a licorice rope on it, a sheet of paper as a mat, and a plastic knife (optional).

Procedure

1 Model how to peel apart three licorice strings from the rope. Have students put one string on the mat to use and return the rest to the paper plate. Students will continue to peel strings as needed throughout the activity.

2 Review basic shapes that your class has been studying (circle, square, rectangle, triangle, and so on).

3 Direct students to use one licorice string to create a shape. For some shapes, students may need to cut the licorice.

4 Walk around the room to check students' work and offer assistance. You might allow students to eat each shape after you have checked it.

MATERIALS

★ thin licorice, such as Twizzlers Pull-n-Peel®

★ paper plates

★ plastic knives (optional; see safety note below)

★ 8½- by 11-inch unlined paper

Safety Note:
If you feel that using plastic knives is problematic, students can pinch the licorice to cut it instead. Demonstrate how to do this at the beginning of the activity.

Building 3-D Shapes

Geometric Shapes

Objective

Students build three-dimensional geometric shapes.

Preparation

- Determine which three-dimensional shapes you would like students to construct in this activity (cube, pyramid, and so on).

- Place $1/2$ cup of soft snack items in a bag for each student.

- You may want to laminate sheets of unlined paper to use as mats for future activities involving food.

- Give each student a bagged snack and a sheet of paper as a mat. Place thin sticks on paper plates for students to share.

Procedure

1 Review the three-dimensional shapes that students have been studying. Remind students that three-dimensional shapes have basic shapes in them. For example, a pyramid has triangles as its sides and a square as its base.

2 Using the soft snack pieces and sticks, construct one of the shapes. Think aloud as you are doing so and ask students for ideas. Show how to insert sticks into a snack piece to form a corner of a shape. Remind students to use the sticks carefully and keep them away from their eyes.

3 Make a list of the shapes you would like students to construct. Have students construct these shapes on their mats. If you allow students to eat their shapes once they have been checked, make sure they have removed the sticks from the snacks first.

MATERIALS

- ★ soft snack, such as marshmallows or gumdrops
- ★ small plastic bags
- ★ pretzel sticks, uncooked spaghetti, small straws, or thin wooden skewers with flat ends
- ★ $8^1/2$- by 11-inch unlined paper

Marshmallow Measurement

Objective

Students measure length using nonstandard units of measure.

Preparation

- Place at least ten marshmallows and twenty mini-marshmallows or $1/4$ cup candy corn in a bag for each student.
- Give each student a bagged snack and a copy of the reproducible.

Procedure

1 Ask students how they would go about measuring the length of an object. Explain that today they will be using an unusual tool to help them measure—marshmallows!

2 Gather students around and model how to line up the marshmallows along a line on the reproducible. Explain that the marshmallows should touch, and determine how they should be placed on the line—side by side or end to end.

3 Explain to students that they will use two sizes of marshmallows to measure the same lines. Discuss how you would like students to handle measurements that are not exact (they might estimate a fraction or round up or down, depending on their skill levels).

4 Instruct students to line up mini-marshmallows on the first line on the sheet, then count and record the number in the first box. Then have students repeat the steps with the larger marshmallows and record the number in the second box. Discuss their findings. Have students measure the other lines in the same way.

MATERIALS

- ★ marshmallows
- ★ mini-marshmallows (or candy corn)
- ★ small plastic bags
- ★ **Measuring Length** reproducible (page 64)

Measuring With Rulers

Objectives

Students measure length using a ruler.
Students place cut lengths in order from shortest to longest.

Preparation

• Provide either inch or centimeter rulers based on your curricular needs. Plastic rulers can be cleaned easily and are best to use in food-related activities.

• You may want to laminate sheets of unlined paper to use as mats for future activities involving food.

• Give each student a paper plate with one or two licorice ropes on it, a ruler, a sheet of paper as a mat, and a plastic knife (optional).

Procedure

1 Model how to peel apart the licorice strands from the rope. Have students carefully separate the strands and set them aside on the paper plate for later use.

2 Discuss the features of the ruler and how to use it. Explain that students will use the ruler to measure the licorice and cut it into pieces of different lengths.

3 Gather students around and model how to lay a piece of licorice along the ruler and cut it to a specific length.

4 Write on the chalkboard the lengths students should use. Once students have finished cutting, have them arrange the pieces in order from shortest to longest on their mats. You might have them write the length beside each piece.

MATERIALS

★ thin licorice, such as Twizzlers Pull-n-Peel®

★ paper plates

★ plastic knives (optional; see safety note below)

★ plastic rulers

★ 8½- by 11-inch unlined paper

Safety Note:
If you feel using plastic knives is problematic, students can pinch the licorice to cut it instead. Demonstrate how to do this at the beginning of the activity.

Measuring Perimeter

Objective

Students measure perimeter using nonstandard units of measure.

Preparation

• Place at least 1/2 cup of snack items in a bag for each student.

• Give each student a bagged snack and a copy of the reproducible.

Procedure

1 Discuss the concept of perimeter, using several examples. Ask students how they might measure the perimeter of an object. Explain that you will be using an unusual tool to measure perimeter—cereal!

2 Point out the shapes on the sheet. Demonstrate how to line up the cereal pieces along the perimeter of one shape so that the pieces are touching one another. Explain that students should count the pieces and record the number in the middle of the shape.

3 Have students work independently to line up cereal pieces along the perimeter of each shape, count them, and record the number of pieces.

4 Once students are finished, invite them to compare results and determine which shapes had the greatest and smallest perimeters.

MATERIALS

★ small, uniform-sized cereal, such as Cheerios®

★ small plastic bags

★ **Perimeter** reproducible (page 65)

Variations

☉ Challenge students to estimate the perimeter of each shape before measuring.

☉ Have students use different snack foods to measure, then compare the results.

Comparing Weights

Objectives

Students estimate the relative weight of objects.
Students measure weight using nonstandard units of measure.

Preparation

- Place at least $1/2$ cup of snack items in a bag for each student.

- Divide the class into groups of five students. Gather a group of five common classroom objects for each group of students.

- Check the balance scales and adjust for accuracy as needed.

- Give each student a bagged snack, an empty plastic bag, and a copy of the reproducible.

- Give each group a set of objects and a balance scale.

Procedure

1 Have students pass the objects around the group to "test" the weight in their hands.

2 Tell students that they will estimate the relative weight of the objects. Explain that this means they will guess which objects weigh more or less than the others. Show students how to record the names of the objects in the first column of the reproducible. They should list them in order of estimated weight, beginning with the lightest and ending with the heaviest.

3 Demonstrate how to weigh one of the objects. Place the object on one side of the balance scale and the empty bag on the other. Place the snack items, one piece at a time, into the empty bag until the scale balances. Have the group count the pieces as you place them on the scale.

MATERIALS

- ★ snack food, such as candy corn or Swedish Fish® (Choose a food that is not too light.)

- ★ small plastic bags

- ★ balance scales

- ★ 5 objects of varying weights (examples: pencil, scissors, eraser)

- ★ **Comparing Weights** reproducible (page 66)

Write the number on the Comparing Weights sheet in the second column beside the name of the object.

4 Have students work in groups to weigh each of the items. Tell students that each group member should get a turn weighing an object. Each group member should then record the findings on his or her sheet.

5 Direct students to rewrite the names of the objects in the third column, this time in the correct order from lightest to heaviest. Have them compare the estimated relative weights with the actual relative weights.

6 Lead a class discussion about the purpose of estimating and the accuracy of estimates.

Comparing Volumes

Length, Weight, and Volume

Objective

Students find and compare the volumes of various containers.

Preparation

- Ask families to donate clean, empty plastic containers such as those for butter, yogurt, or cream cheese. You may want to limit the maximum size to eight ounces.

- Divide the class into small groups. Prepare a set of various containers for each group. Number the containers with a marker.

- Place 1/2 cup of mini-marshmallows in a bag for each student. Each group will need enough marshmallows to fill the largest container.

- Give each group a set of containers. Give each student a bagged snack and a sheet of lined paper.

MATERIALS

- ★ mini-marshmallows
- ★ small plastic bags
- ★ plastic containers (various sizes)
- ★ permanent marker
- ★ lined paper
- ★ pencils

Procedure

1. Explain the concept of volume and talk about ways to measure volume. Ask students to name various objects whose volumes they could measure. Tell students that they will find the volumes of various containers by filling them with marshmallows.

2. Have students record the container numbers on the lined paper. Then instruct students to take turns filling the containers with marshmallows. Explain that they should count the marshmallows and record the number on their paper.

3. Once a group has finished measuring, they should discuss their results and identify the containers with the greatest volume and the least volume. Invite groups to share their findings with the class.

Variations

- ◉ Challenge students to estimate the volume before filling the containers.
- ◉ Have students find volume using other foods, such as popcorn.

Name _____

Date _____

Measuring Length

1 [ ] [ ]

2 [ ] [ ]

3 [ ] [ ]

4 [ ] [ ]

5 [ ] [ ]

Name _____

Date _____

Perimeter

Name _____   Date _____

Comparing Weights

Estimated Relative Weight	Actual Weight	Actual Relative Weight

Time Bingo

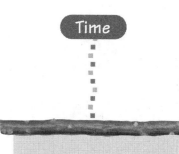

Objective

Students tell time on analog clocks.

Preparation

- Place at least ¼ cup of snack items in a bag for each student.

- Make a copy of the Time Bingo Board for each student. Fill in the times on the clocks (to the hour, half hour, and so on, as prescribed by your curriculum), making sure each card is different. Write these times either on a list or on index cards. Laminate the Bingo boards for greater durability.

- Give each student a bagged snack and a Time Bingo Board.

Procedure

1 Randomly select times from your list (or draw index cards). Call out each time as you write it (12:00, 1:30, and so on) on the chalkboard. If students need more guidance, display each time on a classroom display clock in addition to writing the time on the chalkboard.

2 As you call out each time, students check their boards for an analog clock that shows the same time. If students find a match, they cover the appropriate square with a cracker.

3 When a student has completed a vertical, horizontal, or diagonal row, he or she calls out "Bingo!"

4 Have the student read the time on each clock in the completed row. Check that these times appear on the list on the chalkboard. If the student's answers match, write the student's name on the board for recognition. If not, continue the game.

5 At the end of each game, students can clear their Bingo boards by eating the crackers.

MATERIALS

★ fish-shaped crackers, animal-shaped crackers, or other small snack

★ small plastic bags

★ **Time Bingo Board** reproducible (page 71)

★ classroom display clock (optional)

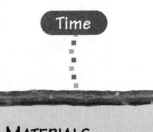

Time

MATERIALS

- ★ pretzel sticks
- ★ classroom display clock
- ★ **Analog Clock** pattern (page 72)
- ★ **Analog Clocks** reproducible (page 73)
- ★ scissors
- ★ paper plates
- ★ glue

Pretzel Clock Hands

Objective

Students draw and move clock hands to show time on an analog clock.

Preparation

- Make a copy of the Analog Clocks reproducible. Beneath the clocks, write eight different times you would like students to work with in this activity. Beside each, write "One hour before" or "One hour after." Make a copy for each student.

- Give each student a copy of the reproducible and Analog Clock pattern, a paper plate, two pretzel sticks, scissors, and glue.

Procedure

1 Have students cut out the Analog Clock pattern and glue it onto the center of the paper plate. Set it aside to dry.

2 While the clocks are drying, place a classroom display clock in the front of the room. Adjust it to a desired time. Discuss the direction the hands on the clock will move if you would like to show either one hour before or one hour after the time displayed. For example, show 2:00 on the display clock. Ask students to describe how the hands will move to show "one hour **after** 2:00" and "one hour **before** 2:00." Provide additional examples until students are ready to work independently.

3 Tell students to bite or break off about half of one of their pretzel sticks. Explain that this will be the hour hand, and the whole pretzel stick will be the minute hand.

4 Model the procedure for students. Read the time shown beneath the first clock on the reproducible. Place the pretzel stick "clock hands" on the Analog Clock pattern to show the same time.

68

5 Read whether you will change the time to one hour before or after the time shown. Adjust the clock hands as necessary, turning them in the correct direction. Draw clock hands to show this new time on the clock face on the reproducible.

6 Once students understand the procedure, have them follow the steps on their own. Walk around the room to check their placement of the pretzel clock hands on their analog clock. Once approved, students can draw clock hands on the reproducible.

7 Students continue until they have completed all eight clock faces.

Variation

Divide the class into three or four teams. Each student needs an analog clock face and pretzel clock hands. Call out a time. All players place their clock hands on their clock to show that time and stand up as soon as they are finished. The first player to stand up earns a point for his or her team if the player's clock shows the correct time. (If incorrect, call out a new time.) Show the correct position on a classroom display clock for students to check their answers. To make this game more challenging, call out a time such as "One hour after 3:30" or "Half an hour after 2:00."

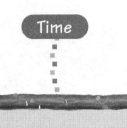

Time

MATERIALS

★ O-shaped cereal, such as Cheerios® (or other small uniform-sized snack)

★ small plastic bags

★ classroom display clock

★ **Digital Clock** reproducible (page 74)

Delicious Digital Times

Objectives

Students read times on an analog clock and represent digital times using edible manipulatives.

Preparation

• Place at least ¼ cup of snack items in a bag for each student. (You may need more depending on the length of the activity.)

• Determine several times for students to show in digital form.

• Give each student a bagged snack and a copy of the reproducible.

Procedure

1 Arrange the hands of a classroom display clock to show a desired time, and place it in the front of the room.

2 Have students use snack items to show the same time in digital form. Demonstrate how to form numbers using snack pieces on the reproducible.

3 Once you have checked students' work, they may clear the clock face.

4 Continue until all times have been displayed.

Digital Clock

70

Name _____   Date _____

Time Bingo Board

Name _____   Date _____

Analog Clock

Analog Clocks

Digital Clock

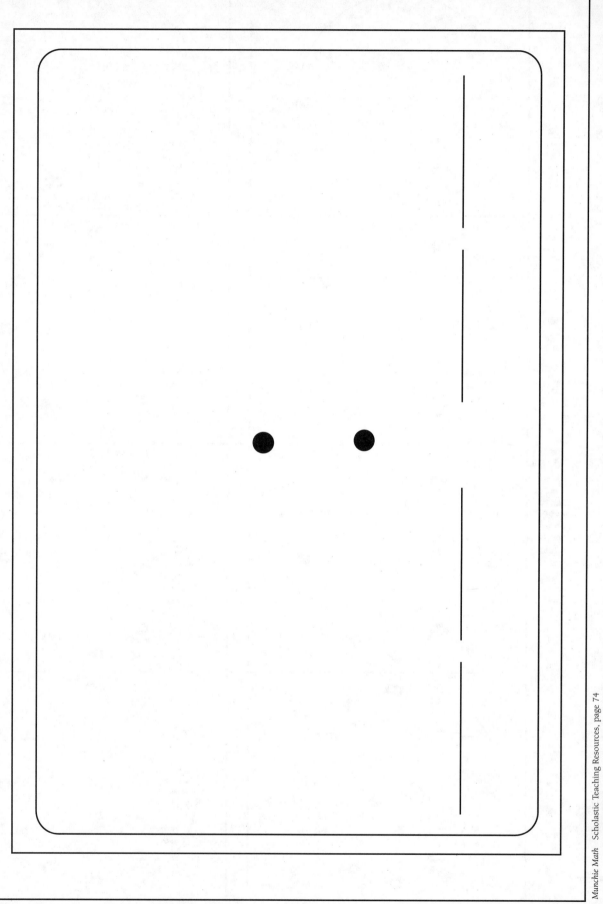

Food Graph

Objective

Students collect and represent data about snacks on a bar graph.

Preparation

- Place ¹/4 cup of snack items in a bag for each student. There should be no more than 15 of each type of snack so that they will fit on the graph.

- Make a copy of one of the Bar Graph reproducibles and fill in the attributes for each bar. For example, label the base of each bar with a color to be sorted. (Both Bar Graph reproducibles allow up to 15 items to be graphed in each bar. Bar Graph 1 features four bars for attributes; Bar Graph 2 features eight bars for attributes.)

- Make a copy of the filled-in graph for each student. If desired, make an overhead transparency of the graph to use in a demonstration.

- Give each student a bagged snack, crayons, and a copy of the reproducible.

Procedure

1. Gather students around or demonstrate the procedure on an overhead projector. Model the way you want students to sort and graph the snack. If you are sorting by color, you might have students color the labels at the base of each bar. Then pull out a few snack items at a time and place them in the appropriate cells on the bar graph. Continue until all the items are used. Show students how to remove a snack item and color in the appropriate cells, one at a time. If sorting by color, color the bars so they match their labels.

2. Once students understand the procedure, have them begin to graph snack items on their own graphs. Some students may need to work with just a few items at a time.

MATERIALS

- ★ cereal or other small snack that can be sorted by attributes*

- ★ small plastic bags

- ★ crayons

- ★ **Bar Graph 1 or 2** reproducible (pages 79–80)

* Multicolored cereal or candies such as Froot Loops®, Skittles®, M&M's®, and jelly beans are all good choices for sorting by color. Lucky Charms® can be sorted by shape. Alpha-Bits® cereal can be sorted by vowels and consonants. For sorting by size, mix different sized cereals or candies.

3 Walk around the room to check students' work and provide assistance. Once you have checked students' placement of snack items, they may remove them and color the cells. Students may eat the removed snacks.

4 Have students continue until they have finished graphing all of their snack items.

Variation

Create a data collection sheet on which students can interpret the data on the bar graph. Make a copy of the sheet for each student. List questions such as:

- Which [attribute] has the most items?
- Which [attribute] has the least items?
- Do any [attributes] have an equal number of items?
- How many more [attribute] items are there than [attribute] items?

Taste-Test Graphing

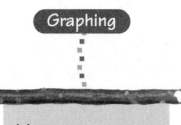

Objective

Students collect and represent data on a bar graph.

Preparation

- Select a food that has several varieties, such as apples or cheese. Gather several different varieties. For example, if using apples, have on hand Golden Delicious, McIntosh, Granny Smith, and so on. If using cheeses, you might include cheddar, Swiss, Brie, provolone, and so on. Be certain students are not allergic to any of the foods.

- Cut the snack into small taste-test pieces and place on a serving dish.

- Make a copy of one of the Bar Graph reproducibles. Write the names of the types of food at the base of each bar. Be certain you have enough spaces for all the children's responses to be recorded. You may need to have each cell represent two students rather than one. Make a copy for each student and make one overhead transparency for the demonstration, if desired.

- Give each student a paper towel or napkin, crayons, and a copy of the reproducible.

MATERIALS

- ★ different kinds of one type of food (for example, apples or cheese)
- ★ paper towels or napkins
- ★ crayons
- ★ **Bar Graph 1 or 2** reproducible (pages 79–80)

Procedure

1. Ask students if they know what a taste test is. Explain the concept and tell students the kind of food they will be tasting (such as apples or cheese). Tell students that this food comes in several varieties and that they will gather and graph information to find out the kind that the class likes best.

2. Distribute the first variety of food to be tasted. Have students wait until everyone is served before tasting.

3 Encourage students to take a small taste of each item. Explain that it is okay to dislike some flavors. Provide students with appropriate responses to disliking the food they taste, such as "I wouldn't choose this one," or "This one tastes sour."

4 Once everyone has tasted a particular kind, ask students to raise their hand if they liked it. Shade that number of boxes in the appropriate column. Have students record the data on their own Bar Graph reproducible.

5 Continue until students have tasted all varieties and you have graphed all responses.

Variation

Create a data collection sheet on which students can interpret the data on the bar graph. Make a copy of the sheet for each student. List questions such as:

- Which food was most popular?
- Which food was least popular?
- Were there any ties?
- How many more people liked [type of food] than [type of food]?

Name _____   Date _____

Bar Graph 1

15			
14			
13			
12			
11			
10			
9			
8			
7			
6			
5			
4			
3			
2			
1			

Number of Items ←

→ **Type of Item**

Bar Graph 2

15							
14							
13							
12							
11							
10							
9							
8							
7							
6							
5							
4							
3							
2							
1							

Number of Items ←

Type of Item →